Epictetus

The Golden Sayings

THE BIG NEST

THE BIG NEST

LONDON · NEW YORK · TORONTO · SAO PAULO · MOSCOW
PARIS · MADRID · BERLIN · ROME · MEXICO CITY · MUMBAI · SEOUL · DOHA
TOKYO · SYDNEY · CAPE TOWN · AUCKLAND · BEIJING

New Edition

Published by The Big Nest

This Edition first published in 2018

Copyright © 2018 The Big Nest

All Rights Reserved.

ISBN: 9781787247147

CONTENTS

THE GOLDEN SAYINGS   7
THE HYMN OF CLEANTHES   93

THE GOLDEN SAYINGS

I

Are these the only works of Providence within us? What words suffice to praise or set them forth? Had we but understanding, should we ever cease hymning and blessing the Divine Power, both openly and in secret, and telling of His gracious gifts? Whether digging or ploughing or eating, should we not sing the hymn to God:—

Great is God, for that He hath given us such instruments to till the ground withal: Great is God, for that He hath given us hands and the power of swallowing and digesting; of unconsciously growing and breathing while we sleep!

Thus should we ever have sung; yea and this, the grandest and divinest hymn of all:—

Great is God, for that He hath given us a mind to apprehend these things, and duly to use them!

What then! seeing that most of you are blinded, should there not be some one to fill this place, and sing the hymn to God on behalf of all men? What else can I that am old and lame do but sing to God? Were I a nightingale, I should do after the manner of a nightingale. Were I a swan, I should do after the manner of a swan. But now, since I am a reasonable being, I must sing to God: that is my work: I do it, nor will I desert this my post, as long as it is granted me to hold it; and upon you too I call to join in this self-same hymn.

II

How then do men act? As though one returning to his

country who had sojourned for the night in a fair inn, should be so captivated thereby as to take up his abode there.

"Friend, thou hast forgotten thine intention! This was not thy destination, but only lay on the way thither."

"Nay, but it is a proper place."

"And how many more of the sort there may be; only to pass through upon thy way! Thy purpose was to return to thy country; to relieve thy kinsmen's fears for thee; thyself to discharge the duties of a citizen; to marry a wife, to beget offspring, and to fill the appointed round of office. Thou didst not come to choose out what places are most pleasant; but rather to return to that wherein thou wast born and where wert appointed to be a citizen."

III

Try to enjoy the great festival of life with other men.

IV

But I have one whom I must please, to whom I must be subject, whom I must obey:—God, and those who come next to Him. He hath entrusted me with myself: He hath made my will subject to myself alone and given me rules for the right use thereof.

V

Rufus used to say, If you have leisure to praise me, what I say is naught. In truth he spoke in such wise, that each of us who sat there, though that some one had accused him to Rufus:—so surely did he lay his finger on the very deeds we did: so surely display the faults of each before his very eyes.

VI

But what saith God?—"Had it been possible, Epictetus, I would have made both that body of thine and thy possessions free and unimpeded, but as it is, be not deceived:—it is not thine own; it is but finely tempered clay. Since then this I could not do, I have given thee a portion of Myself, in the power of desiring and declining and of pursuing and avoiding, and in a word the power of dealing with the things of sense. And if thou neglect not this, but place all that thou hast therein, thou shalt never be let or hindered; thou shalt never lament; thou shalt not blame or flatter any. What then? Seemth this to thee a little thing?"—God forbid!—"Be content then therewith!"

And so I pray the Gods.

VII

What saith Antisthenes? Hast thou never heard?— It is a kingly thing, O Cyrus, to do well and to be evil spoken of.

VIII

"Aye, but to debase myself thus were unworthy of me."

"That," said Epictetus, "is for you to consider, not for me. You know yourself what you are worth in your own eyes; and at what price you will sell yourself. For men sell themselves at various prices. This was why, when Florus was deliberating whether he should appear at Nero's shows, taking part in the performance himself, Agrippinus replied, 'But why do not you appear?' he answered, 'Because I do not even consider the question.' For the man who has once stooped to consider such questions, and to reckon up the value of external things, is not far from forgetting what manner of man he is. Why, what is it that you ask me? Is death preferable, or life? I reply, Life. Pain or pleasure? I reply, Pleasure."

"Well, but if I do not act, I shall lose my head."

"Then go and act! But for my part I will not act."

"Why?"

"Because you think yourself but one among the many threads which make up the texture of the doublet. You should aim at being like men in general—just as your thread has no ambition either to be anything distinguished compared with the other threads. But I desire to be the purple—that small and shining part which makes the rest seem fair and beautiful. Why then do you bid me become even as the multitude? Then were I no longer the purple."

IX

If a man could be throughly penetrated, as he ought, with this thought, that we are all in an especial manner sprung from God, and that God is the Father of men as well as of Gods, full surely he would never conceive aught ignoble or base of himself. Whereas if Cæsar were to adopt you, your haughty looks would be intolerable; will you not be elated at knowing that you are the son of God? Now however it is not so with us: but seeing that in our birth these two things are commingled—the body which we share with the animals, and the Reason and Thought which we share with the Gods, many decline towards this unhappy kinship with the dead, few rise to the blessed kinship with the Divine. Since then every one must deal with each thing according to the view which he forms about it, those few who hold that they are born for fidelity, modesty, and unerring sureness in dealing with the things of sense, never conceive aught base or ignoble of themselves: but the multitude the contrary. Why, what am I?—A wretched human creature; with this miserable flesh of mine. Miserable indeed! but you have something better than that paltry flesh of yours. Why then cling to the one, and neglect the other?

X

Thou art but a poor soul laden with a lifeless body.

XI

The other day I had an iron lamp placed beside my household gods. I heard a noise at the door and on hastening down found my lamp carried off. I reflected that the culprit was in no very strange case. "Tomorrow, my friend," I said, "you will find an earthenware lamp; for a man can only lose what he has."

XII

The reason why I lost my lamp was that the thief was superior to me in vigilance. He paid however this price for the lamp, that in exchange for it he consented to become a thief: in exchange for it, to become faithless.

XIII

But God hath introduced Man to be a spectator of Himself

and of His works; and not a spectator only, but also an interpreter of them. Wherefore it is a shame for man to begin and to leave off where the brutes do. Rather he should begin there, and leave off where Nature leaves off in us: and that is at contemplation, and understanding, and a manner of life that is in harmony with herself.

See then that ye die not without being spectators of these things.

XIV

You journey to Olympia to see the work of Phidias; and each of you holds it a misfortune not to have beheld these things before you die. Whereas when there is no need even to take a journey, but you are on the spot, with the works before you, have you no care to contemplate and study these?

Will you not then perceive either who you are or unto what end you were born: or for what purpose the power of contemplation has been bestowed on you?

"Well, but in life there are some things disagreeable and hard to bear."

And are there none at Olympia? Are you not scorched by the heat? Are you not cramped for room? Have you not to bathe with discomfort? Are you not drenched when it rains? Have you not to endure the clamor and shouting and such annoyances as these? Well, I suppose you set all this over against the splendour of the spectacle and bear it patiently. What then? have you not received greatness of heart, received courage, received fortitude? What care I, if I am great of heart, for aught that can come to pass? What shall cast me down or disturb me? What shall seem painful? Shall I not use the power to the end for which I received it, instead of moaning and wailing over what comes to pass?

XV

If what philosophers say of the kinship of God and Man be true, what remains for men to do but as Socrates did:—never, when asked one's country, to answer, "I am an Athenian or a Corinthian," but "I am a citizen of the world."

XVI

He that hath grasped the administration of the World, who hath learned that this Community, which consists of God and men, is the foremost and mightiest and most comprehensive of all:—that from God have descended the germs of life, not to my father only and father's father, but to all things that are born and grow upon the earth, and in an especial manner to those endowed with Reason (for those only are by their nature fitted to hold communion with God, being by means of Reason conjoined with Him)—why should not such an one call himself a citizen of the world? Why not a son of God? Why should he fear aught that comes to pass among men? Shall kinship with Cæsar, or any other of the great at Rome, be enough to hedge men around with safety and consideration, without a thought of apprehension: while to have God for our Maker, and Father, and Kinsman, shall not this set us free from sorrows and fears?

XVII

I do not think that an old fellow like me need have been sitting here to try and prevent your entertaining abject notions of yourselves, and talking of yourselves in an abject and ignoble way: but to prevent there being by chance among you any such young men as, after recognising their kindred to the Gods, and their bondage in these chains of the body and its manifold necessities, should desire to cast them off as burdens too grievous to be borne, and depart their true kindred. This is the struggle in which your Master and Teacher, were he worthy of the name, should be engaged. You would come to me and say: "Epictetus, we can no longer endure being chained to this wretched body, giving food and drink and rest and purification: aye, and for its sake forced to be subservient to this man and that. Are these not things indifferent and nothing to us? Is it not true that death is no evil? Are we not in a manner kinsmen of the Gods, and have we not come from them? Let us depart thither, whence we came: let us be freed from these chains that confine and press us down. Here are thieves and robbers and tribunals: and they that are called tyrants, who deem that they have after a fashion power over us, because of the miserable body and what appertains to it. Let us show them that they have power over none."

XVIII

And to this I reply:—
"Friends, wait for God. When He gives the signal, and releases you from this service, then depart to Him. But for the present, endure to dwell in the place wherein He hath assigned you your post. Short indeed is the time of your habitation therein, and easy to those that are minded. What tyrant, what robber, what tribunals have any terrors for those who thus esteem the body and all that belong to it as of no account? Stay; depart not rashly hence!"

XIX

Something like that is what should pass between a teacher and ingenuous youths. As it is, what does pass? The teacher is a lifeless body, and you are lifeless bodies yourselves. When you have had enough to eat today, you sit down and weep about tomorrow's food. Slave! if you have it, well and good; if not, you will depart: the door is open—why lament? What further room is there for tears? What further occasion for flattery? Why should one envy another? Why should you stand in awe of them that have much or are placed in power, especially if they be also strong and passionate? Why, what should they do to us? What they can do, we will not regard: what does concern us, that they cannot do. Who then shall rule one that is thus minded?

XX

Seeing this then, and noting well the faculties which you have, you should say,—"Send now, O God, any trial that Thou wilt; lo, I have means and powers given me by Thee to acquit myself with honour through whatever comes to pass!"—No; but there you sit, trembling for fear certain things should come to pass, and moaning and groaning and lamenting over what does come to pass. And then you upbraid the Gods. Such meanness of spirit can have but one result—impiety.

Yet God has not only given us these faculties by means of which we may bear everything that comes to pass without being crushed or depressed thereby; but like a good King and Father, He has given us this without let or hindrance, placed wholly at our own disposition, without reserving to Himself any power of impediment or restraint. Though possessing all these things free and all you own, you do not use them! you do not perceive what it is you have received nor whence it comes, but sit moaning and groaning; some of you blind to the Giver, making no acknowledgment to your Benefactor; others basely giving themselves to complaints and accusations against God.

Yet what faculties and powers you possess for attaining courage and greatness of heart, I can easily show you; what you have for upbraiding and accusation, it is for you to show me!

XXI

How did Socrates bear himself in this regard? How else than as became one who was fully assured that he was the kinsman of Gods?

XXII

If God had made that part of His own nature which He severed from Himself and gave to us, liable to be hindered or constrained either by Himself or any other, He would not have been God, nor would He have been taking care of us as He ought . . . . If you choose, you are free; if you choose, you need blame no man—accuse no man. All things will be at once according to your mind and according to the Mind of God.

XXIII

Petrifaction is of two sorts. There is petrifaction of the understanding; and also of the sense of shame. This happens when a man obstinately refuses to acknowledge plain truths, and persists in maintaining what is self-contradictory. Most of us dread mortification of the body, and would spare no pains to escape anything of that kind. But of mortification of the soul we are utterly heedless. With regard, indeed, to the soul, if a man is in such a state as to be incapable of following or understanding anything, I grant you we do think him in a bad way. But mortification of the sense of shame and modesty we go so far as to dub strength of mind!

XXIV

If we were as intent upon our business as the old fellows

at Rome are upon what interests them, we too might perhaps accomplish something. I know a man older than I am, now Superintendent of the Corn-market at Rome, and I remember when he passed through this place on his way back from exile, what an account he gave me of his former life, declaring that for the future, once home again, his only care should be to pass his remaining years in quiet and tranquility. "For how few years have I left!" he cried. "That," I said, "you will not do; but the moment the scent of Rome is in your nostrils, you will forget it all; and if you can but gain admission to Court, you will be glad enough to elbow your way in, and thank God for it." "Epictetus," he replied, "if ever you find me setting as much as one foot within the Court, think what you will of me."

Well, as it was, what did he do? Ere ever he entered the city, he was met by a despatch from the Emperor. He took it, and forgot the whole of his resolutions. From that moment, he has been piling one thing upon another. I should like to be beside him to remind him of what he said when passing this way, and to add, How much better a prophet I am than you!

What then? do I say man is not made for an active life? Far from it! . . . But there is a great difference between other men's occupations and ours. . . . A glance at theirs will make it clear to you. All day long they do nothing but calculate, contrive, consult how to wring their profit out of food-stuffs, farm-plots and the like. . . . Whereas, I entreat you to learn what the administration of the World is, and what place a Being endowed with reason holds therein: to consider what you are yourself, and wherein your Good and Evil consists.

XXV

A man asked me to write to Rome on his behalf who, as most people thought, had met with misfortune; for having been before wealthy and distinguished, he had afterwards lost all and was living here. So I wrote about him in a humble style. He however on reading the letter returned it to me, with the words: "I asked for your help, not for your pity. No evil has happened unto me."

XXVI

True instruction is this:—to learn to wish that each thing should come to pass as it does. And how does it come to pass? As the Disposer has disposed it. Now He has disposed that there should be summer and winter, and plenty and dearth, and vice and virtue, and all such opposites, for the harmony of the whole.

XXVII

Have this thought ever present with thee, when thou losest any outward thing, what thou gainest in its stead; and if this be the more precious, say not, I have suffered loss.

XXVIII

Concerning the Gods, there are who deny the very existence of the Godhead; others say that it exists, but neither bestirs nor concerns itself nor has forethought for anything. A third party attribute to it existence and forethought, but only for great and heavenly matters, not for anything that is on earth. A fourth party admit things on earth as well as in heaven, but only in general, and not with respect to each individual. A fifth, of whom were Ulysses and Socrates are those that cry:—
I move not without Thy knowledge!

XXIX

Considering all these things, the good and true man submits his judgement to Him that administers the Universe, even as good citizens to the law of the State. And he that is being instructed should come thus minded:—How may I in all things follow the Gods; and, How may I rest satisfied with the Divine Administration; and, How may I become free? For he is free for whom all things come to pass according to his will, and whom none can hinder. What then, is freedom madness? God forbid. For madness and freedom exist not together.

"But I wish all that I desire to come to pass and in the manner that I desire."

—You are mad, you are beside yourself. Know you not that Freedom is a glorious thing and of great worth? But that what I desired at random I should wish at random to come to pass, so far from being noble, may well be exceeding base.

XXX

You must know that it is no easy thing for a principle to become a man's own, unless each day he maintain it and hear it maintained, as well as work it out in life.

XXXI

You are impatient and hard to please. If alone, you call it solitude: if in the company of men, you dub them conspirators and thieves, and find fault with your very parents, children, brothers, and neighbours. Whereas when by yourself you should have called it Tranquillity and Freedom: and herein deemed yourself like unto the Gods. And when in the company of many, you should not have called it a wearisome crowd and tumult, but an assembly and a tribunal; and thus accepted all with contentment.

XXXII

What then is the chastisement of those who accept it not? To be as they are. Is any discontented with being alone? let him be in solitude. Is any discontented with his parents? let him be a bad son, and lament. Is any discontented with his children? let him be a bad father.—"Throw him into prison!"—What prison?—Where he is already: for he is there against his will; and wherever a man is against his will, that to him is a prison. Thus Socrates was not in prison, since he was there with his own consent.

XXXIII

Knowest thou what a speck thou art in comparison with the Universe?—-That is, with respect to the body; since with respect to Reason, thou art not inferior to the Gods, nor less than they. For the greatness of Reason is not measured by length or height, but by the resolves of the mind. Place then thy happiness in that wherein thou art equal to the Gods.

XXXIV

Asked how a man might eat acceptably to the Gods, Epictetus replied:—If when he eats, he can be just, cheerful, equable, temperate, and orderly, can he not thus eat acceptably to the Gods? But when you call for warm water, and your slave does not answer, or when he answers brings it lukewarm, or is not even found to be in the house at all, then not to be vexed nor burst with anger, is not that acceptable to the Gods?

"But how can one endure such people?"

Slave, will you not endure your own brother, that has God to his forefather, even as a son sprung from the same stock, and of the same high descent as yourself? And if you are stationed in a high position, are you therefor forthwith set up for a tyrant? Remember who you are, and whom you rule, that they are by nature your kinsmen, your brothers, the offspring of God.

"But I paid a price for them, not they for me."

Do you see whither you are looking—down to the earth, to the pit, to those despicable laws of the dead? But to the laws of the Gods you do not look.

XXXV

When we are invited to a banquet, we take what is set before us; and were one to call upon his host to set fish upon the table or sweet things, he would be deemed absurd. Yet in a word, we ask the Gods for what they do not give; and that, although they have given us so many things!

XXXVI

Asked how a man might convince himself that every single act of his was under the eye of God, Epictetus answered:—

"Do you not hold that things on earth and things in heaven are continuous and in unison with each other?"

"I do," was the reply.

"Else how should the trees so regularly, as though by God's command, at His bidding flower; at His bidding send forth shoots, bear fruit and ripen it; at His bidding let it fall and shed their leaves, and folded up upon themselves lie in quietness and rest? How else, as the Moon waxes and wanes, as the Sun approaches and recedes, can it be that such vicissitude and alternation is seen in earthly things?

"If then all things that grow, nay, our own bodies, are thus bound up with the whole, is not this still truer of our souls? And if our souls are bound up and in contact with God, as being very parts and fragments plucked from Himself, shall He not feel every movement of theirs as though it were His own, and belonging to His own nature?"

XXXVII

"But," you say, "I cannot comprehend all this at once."

"Why, who told you that your powers were equal to God's?"

Yet God hath placed by the side of each a man's own Guardian Spirit, who is charged to watch over him—a Guardian who sleeps not nor is deceived. For to what better or more watchful Guardian could He have committed which of us? So when you have shut the doors and made a darkness within, remember never to say that you are alone; for you are not alone, but God is within, and your Guardian Spirit, and what light do they need to behold what you do? To this God you also should have sworn allegiance, even as soldiers unto Cæsar. They, when their service is hired, swear to hold the life of Cæsar dearer than all else: and will you not swear your oath, that are deemed worthy of so many and great gifts? And will you not keep your oath when you have sworn it? And what oath will you swear? Never to disobey, never to arraign or murmur at aught that comes to you from His hand: never unwillingly to do or suffer aught that necessity lays upon you.

"Is this oath like theirs?"

They swear to hold no other dearer than Cæsar: you, to hold our true selves dearer than all else beside.

XXXVIII

"How shall my brother cease to be wroth with me?"

Bring him to me, and I will tell him. But to thee I have

nothing to say about his anger.

XXXIX

When one took counsel of Epictetus, saying, "What I seek is this, how even though my brother be not reconciled to me, I may still remain as Nature would have me to be," he replied: "All great things are slow of growth; nay, this is true even of a grape or of a fig. If then you say to me now, I desire a fig, I shall answer, It needs time: wait till it first flower, then cast its blossom, then ripen. Whereas then the fruit of the fig-tree reaches not maturity suddenly nor yet in a single hour, do you nevertheless desire so quickly, and easily to reap the fruit of the mind of man?—Nay, expect it not, even though I bade you!"

XL

Epaphroditus had a shoemaker whom he sold as being good-for-nothing. This fellow, by some accident, was afterwards purchased by one of Cæsar's men, and became a shoemaker to Cæsar. You should have seen what respect Epaphroditus paid him then. "How does the good Felicion? Kindly let me know!" And if any of us inquired, "What is Epaphroditus doing?" the answer was, "He is consulting about so and so with Felicion."—Had he not sold him as good-for-nothing? Who had in a trice converted him into a wiseacre?

This is what comes of holding of importance anything but the things that depend on the Will.

XLI

What you shun enduring yourself, attempt not to impose on others. You shun slavery—beware of enslaving others! If you can endure to do that, one would think you had been once upon a time a slave yourself. For Vice has nothing in common with virtue, nor Freedom with slavery.

XLII

Has a man been raised to tribuneship? Every one that he meets congratulates him. One kisses him on the eyes, another on the neck, while the slaves kiss his hands. He goes home to find torches burning; he ascends to the Capitol to sacrifice.—Who ever sacrificed for having had right desires; for having conceived such inclinations as Nature would have him? In truth we thank the Gods for that wherein we place our happiness.

XLIII

A man was talking to me to-day about the priesthood of Augustus. I said to him, "Let the thing go, my good Sir; you will spend a good deal to no purpose."

"Well, but my name will be inserted in all documents and contracts."

"Will you be standing there to tell those that read them, That is my name written there? And even if you could now be there in every case, what will you do when you are dead?"

"At all events my name will remain."

"Inscribe it on a stone and it will remain just as well. And think, beyond Nicopolis what memory of you will there be?"

"But I shall have a golden wreath to wear."

"If you must have a wreath, get a wreath of roses and put it on; you will look more elegant!"

XLIV

Above all, remember that the door stands open. Be not more fearful than children; but as they, when they weary of the game, cry, "I will play no more," even so, when thou art in the like case, cry, "I will play no more" and depart. But if thou stayest, make no lamentation.

XLV

Is there smoke in the room? If it be slight, I remain; if grievous, I quit it. For you must remember this and hold it fast, that the door stands open.
"You shall not dwell at Nicopolis!"
Well and good.
"Nor at Athens."
Then I will not dwell at Athens either.
"Nor at Rome."
Nor at Rome either.
"You shall dwell in Gyara!"
Well: but to dwell in Gyara seems to me like a grievous smoke; I depart to a place where none can forbid me to dwell: that habitation is open unto all! As for the last garment of all, that is the poor body; beyond that, none can do aught unto me. This why Demetrius said to Nero: "You threaten me with death; it is Nature who threatens you!"

XLVI

The beginning of philosophy is to know the condition of one's own mind. If a man recognises that this is in a weakly state, he will not then want to apply it to questions of the greatest moment. As it is, men who are not fit to swallow even a morsel, buy whole treatises and try to devour them. Accordingly they either vomit them up again, or suffer from indigestion, whence come gripings, fluxions, and fevers. Whereas they should have stopped to consider their capacity.

XLVII

In theory it is easy to convince an ignorant person: in actual life, men not only object to offer themselves to be convinced, but hate the man who has convinced them. Whereas Socrates used to say that we should never lead a life not subjected to examination.

XLVIII

This is the reason why Socrates, when reminded that he should prepare for his trial, answered: "Thinkest thou not that I have been preparing for it all my life?"
"In what way?"
"I have maintained that which in me lay!"
"How so?"
"I have never, secretly or openly, done a wrong unto any."

XLIX

In what character dost thou now come forward?
As a witness summoned by God. "Come thou," saith God, "and testify for me, for thou art worthy of being brought forward as a witness by Me. Is aught that is outside thy will either good or bad? Do I hurt any man? Have I placed the good of each

in the power of any other than himself? What witness dost thou bear to God?"

"I am in evil state, Master, I am undone! None careth for me, none giveth me aught: all men blame, all speak evil of me."

Is this the witness thou wilt bear, and do dishonour to the calling wherewith He hath called thee, because He hath done thee so great honour, and deemed thee worthy of being summoned to bear witness in so great a cause?

L

Wouldst thou have men speak good of thee? speak good of them. And when thou hast learned to speak good of them, try to do good unto them, and thus thou wilt reap in return their speaking good of thee.

LI

When thou goest in to any of the great, remember that Another from above sees what is passing, and that thou shouldst please Him rather than man. He therefore asks thee:—

"In the Schools, what didst thou call exile, imprisonment, bonds, death and shame?"

"I called them things indifferent."

"What then dost thou call them now? Are they at all changed?"

"No."

"Is it then thou that art changed?"

"No."

"Say then, what are things indifferent?"

"Things that are not in our power."

"Say then, what follows?"

"That things which are not in our power are nothing to me."

"Say also what things you hold to be good."

"A will such as it ought to be, and a right use of the things of sense."

"And what is the end?"
"To follow Thee!"

LII

"That Socrates should ever have been so treated by the Athenians!"

Slave! why say "Socrates"? Speak of the thing as it is: That ever then the poor body of Socrates should have been dragged away and haled by main force to prison! That ever hemlock should have been given to the body of Socrates; that that should have breathed its life away!—Do you marvel at this? Do you hold this unjust? Is it for this that you accuse God? Had Socrates no compensation for this? Where then for him was the ideal Good? Whom shall we hearken to, you or him? And what says he?

"Anytus and Melitus may put me to death: to injure me is beyond their power."

And again:—

"If such be the will of God, so let it be."

LIII

Nay, young man, for heaven's sake; but once thou hast heard these words, go home and say to thyself:—"It is not Epictetus that has told me these things: how indeed should he? No, it is some gracious God through him. Else it would never have entered his head to tell me them—he that is not used to speak to any one thus. Well, then, let us not lie under the wrath of God, but be obedient unto Him."—-Nay, indeed; but if a raven by its croaking bears thee any sign, it is not the raven but God that sends the sign through the raven; and if He signifies anything to thee through human voice, will He not cause the man to say these words to thee, that thou mayest know the power of the

Divine—how He sends a sign to some in one way and to others in another, and on the greatest and highest matters of all signifies His will through the noblest messenger?

What else does the poet mean:—

I spake unto him erst Myself, and sent
Hermes the shining One, to check and warn him,
The husband not to slay, nor woo the wife!

LIV

In the same way my friend Heraclitus, who had a trifling suit about a petty farm at Rhodes, first showed the judges that his cause was just, and then at the finish cried, "I will not entreat you: nor do I care what sentence you pass. It is you who are on your trial, not I!"—And so he ended the case.

LV

As for us, we behave like a herd of deer. When they flee from the huntsman's feathers in affright, which way do they turn? What haven of safety do they make for? Why, they rush upon the nets! And thus they perish by confounding what they should fear with that wherein no danger lies. . . . Not death or pain is to be feared, but the fear of death or pain. Well said the poet therefore:—

Death has no terror; only a Death of shame!

LVI

How is it then that certain external things are said to be natural, and other contrary to Nature?

Why, just as it might be said if we stood alone and apart from others. A foot, for instance, I will allow it is natural should be clean. But if you take it as a foot, and as a thing which does not stand by itself, it will beseem it (if need be) to walk in the mud, to tread on thorns, and sometimes even to be cut off, for the benefit of the whole body; else it is no longer a foot. In some such way we should conceive of ourselves also. What art thou?—A man.—Looked at as standing by thyself and separate, it is natural for thee in health and wealth long to live. But looked at as a Man, and only as a part of a Whole, it is for that Whole's sake that thou shouldest at one time fall sick, at another brave the perils of the sea, again, know the meaning of want and perhaps die an early death. Why then repine? Knowest thou not that as the foot is no more a foot if detached from the body, so thou in like case art no longer a Man? For what is a Man? A part of a City:—first of the City of Gods and Men; next, of that which ranks nearest it, a miniature of the universal City. . . . In such a body, in such a world enveloping us, among lives like these, such things must happen to one or another. Thy part, then, being here, is to speak of these things as is meet, and to order them as befits the matter.

LVII

That was a good reply which Diogenes made to a man who asked him for letters of recommendation.—"That you are a man, he will know when he sees you;—whether a good or bad one, he will know if he has any skill in discerning the good or bad. But if he has none, he will never know, though I write him a thousand times."—It is as though a piece of silver money desired to be recommended to some one to be tested. If the man be a good judge of silver, he will know: the coin will tell its own tale.

LVIII

Even as the traveller asks his way of him that he meets, inclined in no wise to bear to the right rather than to the left (for he desires only the way leading whither he would go), so should we come unto God as to a guide; even as we use our eyes without admonishing them to show us some things rather than others, but content to receive the images of such things as they present to us. But as it is we stand anxiously watching the victim, and with the voice of supplication call upon the augur:—"Master, have mercy on me: vouchsafe unto me a way of escape!" Slave, would you then have aught else then what is best? is there anything better than what is God's good pleasure? Why, as far as in you lies, would you corrupt your Judge, and lead your Counsellor astray?

LIX

God is beneficent. But the Good also is beneficent. It should seem then that where the real nature of God is, there too is to be found the real nature of the Good. What then is the real nature of God?—Intelligence, Knowledge, Right Reason. Here then without more ado seek the real nature of the Good. For surely thou dost not seek it in a plant or in an animal that reasoneth not.

LX

Seek then the real nature of the Good in that without whose presence thou wilt not admit the Good to exist in aught else.— What then? Are not these other things also works of God?—They are; but not preferred to honour, nor are they portions of God. But thou art a thing preferred to honour: thou art thyself a fragment torn from God:—thou hast a portion of Him within thyself. How is it then that thou dost not know thy high descent—dost not know whence thou comest? When thou eatest, wilt thou not remember who thou art that eatest and whom thou feedest? In intercourse, in exercise, in discussion knowest thou not that it is a God whom thou feedest, a God whom thou exercisest, a God whom thou bearest about with thee, O miserable! and thou perceivest it not. Thinkest thou that I speak of a God of silver or gold, that is without thee? Nay, thou bearest Him within thee! all unconscious of polluting Him with thoughts impure and unclean deeds. Were an image of God present, thou wouldest not dare to act as thou dost, yet, when God Himself is present within thee, beholding and hearing all, thou dost not blush to think such thoughts and do such deeds, O thou that art insensible of thine own nature and liest under the wrath of God!

LXI

Why then are we afraid when we send a young man from the Schools into active life, lest he should indulge his appetites intemperately, lest he should debase himself by ragged clothing, or be puffed up by fine raiment? Knows he not the God within him; knows he not with whom he is starting on his way? Have we patience to hear him say to us, Would I had thee with me!— Hast thou not God where thou art, and having Him dost thou still seek for any other! Would He tell thee aught else than these things? Why, wert thou a statue of Phidias, an Athena or a Zeus, thou wouldst bethink thee both of thyself and thine artificer; and hadst thou any sense, thou wouldst strive to do no dishonour to thyself or him that fashioned thee, nor appear to beholders in unbefitting guise. But now, because God is thy Maker, is that why thou carest not of what sort thou shalt show thyself to be? Yet how different the artists and their workmanship! What human artist's work, for example, has in it the faculties that are displayed in fashioning it? Is it aught but marble, bronze, gold, or ivory? Nay, when the Athena of Phidias has put forth her hand and received therein a Victory, in that attitude she stands for evermore. But God's works move and breathe; they use and judge the things of sense. The workmanship of such an Artist, wilt thou dishonor Him? Ay, when he not only fashioned thee, but placed thee, like a ward, in the care and guardianship of thyself alone, wilt thou not only forget this, but also do dishonour to what is committed to thy care! If God had entrusted thee with an orphan, wouldst thou have thus neglected him? He hath delivered thee to thine own care, saying, I had none more faithful than myself: keep this man for me such as Nature hath made him—modest, faithful, high-minded, a stranger to fear, to passion, to perturbation....

Such will I show myself to you all.—"What, exempt from sickness also: from age, from death?"—Nay, but accepting sickness, accepting death as becomes a God!

LXII

No labour, according to Diogenes, is good but that which aims at producing courage and strength of soul rather than of body.

LXIII

A guide, on finding a man who has lost his way, brings him back to the right path—he does not mock and jeer at him and then take himself off. You also must show the unlearned man the truth, and you will see that he will follow. But so long as you do not show it him, you should not mock, but rather feel your own incapacity.

LXIV

It was the first and most striking characteristic of Socrates never to become heated in discourse, never to utter an injurious or insulting word—on the contrary, he persistently bore insult from others and thus put an end to the fray. If you care to know the extent of his power in this direction, read Xenophon's Banquet, and you will see how many quarrels he put an end to. This is why the Poets are right in so highly commending this faculty:—

Quickly and wisely withal even bitter feuds would he settle.

Nevertheless the practice is not very safe at present, especially in Rome. One who adopts it, I need not say, ought not to carry it out in an obscure corner, but boldly accost, if occasion serve, some personage of rank or wealth.

"Can you tell me, sir, to whose care you entrust your horses?"

"I can."

"Is it to the first comer, who knows nothing about them?"

"Certainly not."

"Well, what of the man who takes care of your gold, your silver or your raiment?"

"He must be experienced also."

"And your body—have you ever considered about entrusting it to any one's care?"

"Of course I have."

"And no doubt to a person of experience as a trainer, a physician?"

"Surely."

"And these things the best you possess, or have you anything more precious?"

"What can you mean?"

"I mean that which employs these; which weights all things; which takes counsel and resolve."

"Oh, you mean the soul."

"You take me rightly; I do mean the soul. By Heaven, I hold that far more precious than all else I possess. Can you show me then what care you bestow on a soul? For it can scarcely be thought that a man of your wisdom and consideration in the city would suffer your most precious possession to go to ruin through carelessness and neglect."

"Certainly not."

"Well, do you take care of it yourself? Did any one teach you the right method, or did you discover it yourself?"

Now here comes in the danger: first, that the great man may

answer, "Why, what is that to you, my good fellow? are you my master?" And then, if you persist in troubling him, may raise his hand to strike you. It is a practice of which I was myself a warm admirer until such experiences as these befell me.

LXV

When a youth was giving himself airs in the Theatre and saying, "I am wise, for I have conversed with many wise men," Epictetus replied, "I too have conversed with many rich men, yet I am not rich!"

LXVI

We see that a carpenter becomes a carpenter by learning certain things: that a pilot, by learning certain things, becomes a pilot. Possibly also in the present case the mere desire to be wise and good is not enough. It is necessary to learn certain things. This is then the object of our search. The Philosophers would have us first learn that there is a God, and that His Providence directs the Universe; further, that to hide from Him not only one's acts but even one's thoughts and intentions is impossible; secondly, what the nature of God is. Whatever that nature is discovered to be, the man who would please and obey Him must strive with all his might to be made like unto him. If the Divine is faithful, he also must be faithful; if free, he also must be free; if beneficent, he also must be beneficent; if magnanimous, he also must be magnanimous. Thus as an imitator of God must he follow Him in every deed and word.

LXVII

If I show you, that you lack just what is most important and necessary to happiness, that hitherto your attention has been bestowed on everything rather than that which claims it most; and, to crown all, that you know neither what God nor Man is—neither what Good or Evil is: why, that you are ignorant of everything else, perhaps you may bear to be told; but to hear that you know nothing of yourself, how could you submit to that? How could you stand your ground and suffer that to be proved? Clearly not at all. You instantly turn away in wrath. Yet what harm have I done to you? Unless indeed the mirror harms the ill-favoured man by showing him to himself just as he is; unless the physician can be thought to insult his patient, when he tells him:—"Friend, do you suppose there is nothing wrong with you? why, you have a fever. Eat nothing to-day, and drink only water." Yet no one says, "What an insufferable insult!" Whereas if you say to a man, "Your desires are inflamed, your instincts of rejection are weak and low, your aims are inconsistent, your impulses are not in harmony with Nature, your opinions are rash and false," he forthwith goes away and complains that you have insulted him.

LXVIII

Our way of life resembles a fair. The flocks and herds are passing along to be sold, and the greater part of the crowd to buy and sell. But there are some few who come only to look at the fair, to inquire how and why it is being held, upon what authority and with what object. So too, in this great Fair of life, some, like the cattle, trouble themselves about nothing but the fodder. Know all of you, who are busied about land, slaves and public posts, that these are nothing but fodder! Some few there are attending the Fair, who love to contemplate what the world is, what He that administers it. Can there be no Administrator? is it possible, that while neither city nor household could endure even a moment without one to administer and see to its welfare, this Fabric, so fair, so vast, should be administered in order so harmonious, without a purpose and by blind chance? There is therefore an Administrator. What is His nature and how does He administer? And who are we that are His children and what work were we born to perform? Have we any close connection or relation with Him or not?

Such are the impressions of the few of whom I speak. And further, they apply themselves solely to considering and examining the great assembly before they depart. Well, they are derided by the multitude. So are the lookers-on by the traders: aye, and if the beasts had any sense, they would deride those who thought much of anything but fodder!

LXIX

I think I know now what I never knew before—the meaning of the common saying, A fool you can neither bend nor break. Pray heaven I may never have a wise fool for my friend! There is nothing more intractable.—"My resolve is fixed!"—Why so madman say too; but the more firmly they believe in their delusions, the more they stand in need of treatment.

LXX

—"O! when shall I see Athens and its Acropolis again?"—Miserable man! art thou not contented with the daily sights that meet thine eyes? canst thou behold aught greater or nobler than the Sun, Moon, and Stars; than the outspread Earth and Sea? If indeed thou apprehendest Him who administers the universe, if thou bearest Him about within thee, canst thou still hanker after mere fragments of stone and fine rock? When thou art about to bid farewell to the Sun and Moon itself, wilt thou sit down and cry like a child? Why, what didst thou hear, what didst thou learn? why didst thou write thyself down a philosopher, when thou mightest have written what was the fact, namely, "I have made one or two Compendiums, I have read some works of Chrysippus, and I have not even touched the hem of Philosophy's robe!"

LXXI

Friend, lay hold with a desperate grasp, ere it is too late, on Freedom, on Tranquility, on Greatness of soul! Lift up thy head, as one escaped from slavery; dare to look up to God, and say:—"Deal with me henceforth as Thou wilt; Thou and I are of one mind. I am Thine: I refuse nothing that seeeth good to Thee; lead on whither Thou wilt; clothe me in what garb Thou pleasest; wilt Thou have me a ruler or a subject—at home or in exile—poor or rich? All these things will I justify unto men for Thee. I will show the true nature of each. . . ."

Who would Hercules have been had he loitered at home? no Hercules, but Eurystheus. And in his wanderings through the world how many friends and comrades did he find? but nothing dearer to him than God. Wherefore he was believed to be God's son, as indeed he was. So then in obedience to Him, he went about delivering the earth from injustice and lawlessness.

But thou art not Hercules, thou sayest, and canst not deliver others from their iniquity—not even Theseus, to deliver the soil of Attica from its monsters? Purge away thine own, cast forth thence—from thine own mind, not robbers and monsters, but Fear, Desire, Envy, Malignity, Avarice, Effeminacy, Intemperance. And these may not be cast out, except by looking to God alone, by fixing thy affections on Him only, and by consecrating thyself to His commands. If thou choosest aught else, with sighs and groans thou wilt be forced to follow a Might greater than thine own, ever seeking Tranquillity without, and never able to attain unto her. For thou seekest her where she is not to be found; and where she is, there thou seekest her not!

LXXII

If a man would pursue Philosophy, his first task is to throw away conceit. For it is impossible for a man to begin to learn what he has a conceit that he already knows.

LXXIII

Give me but one young man, that has come to the School with this intention, who stands forth a champion of this cause, and says, "All else I renounce, content if I am but able to pass my life free from hindrance and trouble; to raise my head aloft and face all things as a free man; to look up to heaven as a friend of God, fearing nothing that may come to pass!" Point out such a one to me, that I may say, "Enter, young man, into possession of that which is thine own. For thy lot is to adorn Philosophy. Thine are these possessions; thine these books, these discourses!"

And when our champion has duly exercised himself in this part of the subject, I hope he will come back to me and say:—"What I desire is to be free from passion and from perturbation; as one who grudges no pains in the pursuit of piety and philosophy, what I desire is to know my duty to the Gods, my duty to my parents, to my brothers, to my country, to strangers."

"Enter then on the second part of the subject; it is thine also."

"But I have already mastered the second part; only I wished to stand firm and unshaken—as firm when asleep as when awake, as firm when elated with wine as in despondency and dejection."

"Friend, you are verily a God! you cherish great designs."

LXXIV

"The question at stake," said Epictetus, "is no common one; it is this:—Are we in our senses, or are we not?"

LXXV

If you have given way to anger, be sure that over and above the evil involved therein, you have strengthened the habit, and added fuel to the fire. If overcome by a temptation of the flesh, do not reckon it a single defeat, but that you have also strengthened your dissolute habits. Habits and faculties are necessarily affected by the corresponding acts. Those that were not there before, spring up: the rest gain in strength and extent. This is the account which Philosophers give of the origin of diseases of the mind:—Suppose you have once lusted after money: if reason sufficient to produce a sense of evil be applied, then the lust is checked, and the mind at once regains its original authority; whereas if you have recourse to no remedy, you can no longer look for this return—on the contrary, the next time it is excited by the corresponding object, the flame of desire leaps up more quickly than before. By frequent repetition, the mind in the long run becomes callous; and thus this mental disease produces confirmed Avarice.

One who has had fever, even when it has left him, is not in the same condition of health as before, unless indeed his cure is complete. Something of the same sort is true also of diseases of the mind. Behind, there remains a legacy of traces and blisters: and unless these are effectually erased, subsequent blows on the same spot will produce no longer mere blisters, but sores. If you do not wish to be prone to anger, do not feed the habit; give it nothing which may tend its increase. At first, keep quiet and count the days when you were not angry: "I used to be angry every day, then every other day: next every two, next every three days!" and if you succeed in passing thirty days, sacrifice to the Gods in thanksgiving.

LXXVI

How then may this be attained?—Resolve, now if never before, to approve thyself to thyself; resolve to show thyself fair in God's sight; long to be pure with thine own pure self and God!

LXXVII

That is the true athlete, that trains himself to resist such outward impressions as these.

"Stay, wretched man! suffer not thyself to be carried away!" Great is the combat, divine the task! you are fighting for Kingship, for Liberty, for Happiness, for Tranquillity. Remember God: call upon Him to aid thee, like a comrade that stands beside thee in the fight.

LXXVIII

Who then is a Stoic—in the sense that we call a statue of Phidias which is modelled after that master's art? Show me a man in this sense modelled after the doctrines that are ever upon his lips. Show me a man that is sick—and happy; an exile—and happy; in evil report—and happy! Show me him, I ask again. So help me Heaven, I long to see one Stoic! Nay, if you cannot show me one fully modelled, let me at least see one in whom the process is at work—one whose bent is in that direction. Do me that favour! Grudge it not to an old man, to behold a sight he has never yet beheld. Think you I wish to see the Zeus or Athena of Phidias, bedecked with gold and ivory?—Nay, show me, one of you, a human soul, desiring to be of one mind with God, no more to lay blame on God or man, to suffer nothing to disappoint, nothing to cross him, to yield neither to anger, envy, nor jealousy—in a word, why disguise the matter? one that from a man would fain become a God; one that while still imprisoned in this dead body makes fellowship with God his aim. Show me him!—Ah, you cannot! Then why mock yourselves and delude others? why stalk about tricked out in other men's attire, thieves and robbers that you are of names and things to which you can show no title!

LXXIX

If you have assumed a character beyond your strength, you have both played a poor figure in that, and neglected one that is within your powers.

LXXX

Fellow, you have come to blows at home with a slave: you have turned the household upside down, and thrown the neighbourhood into confusion; and do you come to me then with airs of assumed modesty—do you sit down like a sage and criticise my explanation of the readings, and whatever idle babble you say has come into my head? Have you come full of envy, and dejected because nothing is sent you from home; and while the discussion is going on, do you sit brooding on nothing but how your father or your brother are disposed towards you:—"What are they saying about me there? at this moment they imagine I am making progress and saying, He will return perfectly omniscient! I wish I could become omniscient before I return; but that would be very troublesome. No one sends me anything—the baths at Nicopolis are dirty; things are wretched at home and wretched here." And then they say, "Nobody is any the better for the School."—Who comes to the School with a sincere wish to learn: to submit his principles to correction and himself to treatment? Who, to gain a sense of his wants? Why then be surprised if you carry home from the School exactly what you bring into it?

LXXXI

"Epictetus, I have often come desiring to hear you speak, and you have never given me any answer; now if possible, I entreat you, say something to me."

"Is there, do you think," replied Epictetus, "an art of speaking as of other things, if it is to be done skilfully and with profit to the hearer?"

"Yes."

"And are all profited by what they hear, or only some among them? So that it seems there is an art of hearing as well as of speaking. . . . To make a statue needs skill: to view a statue aright needs skill also."

"Admitted."

"And I think all will allow that one who proposes to hear philosophers speak needs a considerable training in hearing. Is that not so? The tell me on what subject your are able to hear me."

"Why, on good and evil."

"The good and evil of what? a horse, an ox?"

"No; of a man."

"Do we know then what Man is? what his nature is? what is the idea we have of him? And are our ears practised in any degree on the subject? Nay, do you understand what Nature is? can you follow me in any degree when I say that I shall have to use demonstration? Do you understand what Demonstration is? what True or False is? . . . must I drive you to Philosophy? . . . Show me what good I am to do by discoursing with you. Rouse my desire to do so. The sight of a pasture it loves stirs in a sheep the desire to feed: show it a stone or a bit of bread and it remains unmoved. Thus we also have certain natural desires, aye, and one that moves us to speak when we find a listener that is worth his salt: one that himself stirs the spirit. But if he sits by like a stone or a tuft of grass, how can he rouse a man's desire?"

"Then you will say nothing to me?"

"I can only tell you this: that one who knows not who he is and to what end he was born; what kind of world this is and with whom he is associated therein; one who cannot distinguish Good and Evil, Beauty and Foulness, . . . Truth and Falsehood, will never follow Reason in shaping his desires and impulses and repulsions, nor yet in assent, denial, or suspension of judgement; but will in one word go about deaf and blind, thinking himself to be somewhat, when he is in truth of no account. Is there anything new in all this? Is not this ignorance the cause of all the mistakes and mischances of men since the human race began? . . ."

"This is all I have to say to you, and even this against the grain. Why? Because you have not stirred my spirit. For what can I see in you to stir me, as a spirited horse will stir a judge of horses? Your body? That you maltreat. Your dress? That is luxurious. You behavior, your look?—Nothing whatever. When you want to hear a philosopher, do not say, You say nothing to me'; only show yourself worthy or fit to hear, and then you will see how you will move the speaker."

LXXXII

And now, when you see brothers apparently good friends and living in accord, do not immediately pronounce anything upon their friendship, though they should affirm it with an oath, though they should declare, "For us to live apart in a thing impossible!" For the heart of a bad man is faithless, unprincipled, inconstant: now overpowered by one impression, now by another. Ask not the usual questions, Were they born of the same parents, reared together, and under the same tutor; but ask this only, in what they place their real interest—whether in outward things or in the Will. If in outward things, call them not friends, any more than faithful, constant, brave or free: call them not even human beings, if you have any sense. . . . But should you hear that these men hold the Good to lie only in the Will, only in rightly dealing with the things of sense, take no more trouble to inquire whether they are father and son or brothers, or comrades of long standing; but, sure of this one thing, pronounce as boldly that they are friends as that they are faithful and just: for where else can Friendship be found than where Modesty is, where there is an interchange of things fair and honest, and of such only?

LXXXIII

No man can rob us of our Will—no man can lord it over that!

LXXXIV

When disease and death overtake me, I would fain be found engaged in the task of liberating mine own Will from the assaults of passion, from hindrance, from resentment, from slavery.

Thus would I fain to be found employed, so that I may say to God, "Have I in aught transgressed Thy commands? Have I in aught perverted the faculties, the senses, the natural principles that Thou didst give me? Have I ever blamed Thee or found fault with Thine administration? When it was Thy good pleasure, I fell sick—and so did other men: by my will consented. Because it was Thy pleasure, I became poor: but my heart rejoiced. No power in the State was mine, because Thou wouldst not: such power I never desired! Hast Thou ever seen me of more doleful countenance on that account? Have I not ever drawn nigh unto Thee with cheerful look, waiting upon Thy commands, attentive to Thy signals? Wilt Thou that I now depart from the great Assembly of men? I go: I give Thee all thanks, that Thou hast deemed me worthy to take part with Thee in this Assembly: to behold Thy works, to comprehend this Thine administration."

Such I would were the subject of my thoughts, my pen, my study, when death overtakes me.

LXXXV

Seemeth it nothing to you, never to accuse, never to blame either God or Man? to wear ever the same countenance in going forth as in coming in? This was the secret of Socrates: yet he never said that he knew or taught anything. . . . Who amongst you makes this his aim? Were it indeed so, you would gladly endure sickness, hunger, aye, death itself.

LXXXVI

How are we constituted by Nature? To be free, to be noble, to be modest (for what other living thing is capable of blushing, or of feeling the impression of shame?) and to subordinate pleasure to the ends for which Nature designed us, as a handmaid and a minister, in order to call forth our activity; in order to keep us constant to the path prescribed by Nature.

LXXXVII

The husbandman deals with land; physicians and trainers with the body; the wise man with his own Mind.

LXXXVIII

Which of us does not admire what Lycurgus the Spartan did? A young citizen had put out his eye, and been handed over to him by the people to be punished at his own discretion. Lycurgus abstained from all vengeance, but on the contrary instructed and made a good man of him. Producing him in public in the theatre, he said to the astonished Spartans:—"I received this young man at your hands full of violence and wanton insolence; I restore him to you in his right mind and fit to serve his country."

LXXXIX

A money-changer may not reject Cæsar's coin, nor may the seller of herbs, but must when once the coin is shown, deliver what is sold for it, whether he will or no. So is it also with the Soul. Once the Good appears, it attracts towards itself; evil repels. But a clear and certain impression of the Good the Soul will never reject, any more than men do Cæsar's coin. On this hangs every impulse alike of Man and God.

XC

Asked what Common Sense was, Epictetus replied:—
As that may be called a Common Ear which distinguishes only sounds, while that which distinguishes musical notes is not common but produced by training; so there are certain things which men not entirely perverted see by the natural principles common to all. Such a constitution of the Mind is called Common Sense.

XCI

Canst thou judge men? . . . then make us imitators of thyself, as Socrates did. Do this, do not do that, else will I cast thee into prison; this is not governing men like reasonable creatures. Say rather, As God hath ordained, so do; else thou wilt suffer chastisement and loss. Askest thou what loss? None other than this: To have left undone what thou shouldst have done: to have lost the faithfulness, the reverence, the modesty that is in thee!

Greater loss than this seek not to find!

XCII

"His son is dead."
What has happened?
"His son is dead."
Nothing more?
"Nothing."
"His ship is lost."
"He has been haled to prison."
What has happened?
"He has been haled to prison."
But that any of these things are misfortunes to him, is an addition which every one makes of his own. But (you say) God is unjust is this.—Why? For having given thee endurance and greatness of soul? For having made such things to be no evils? For placing happiness within thy reach, even when enduring them? For open unto thee a door, when things make not for thy good?—Depart, my friend and find fault no more!

XCIII

You are sailing to Rome (you tell me) to obtain the post of Governor of Cnossus. You are not content to stay at home with the honours you had before; you want something on a larger scale, and more conspicuous. But when did you ever undertake a voyage for the purpose of reviewing your own principles and getting rid of any of them that proved unsound? Whom did you ever visit for that object? What time did you ever set yourself for that? What age? Run over the times of your life—by yourself, if you are ashamed before me. Did you examine your principles when a boy? Did you not do everything just as you do now? Or when you were a stripling, attending the school of oratory and practising the art yourself, what did you ever imagine you lacked? And when you were a young man, entered upon public life, and were pleading causes and making a name, who any longer seemed equal to you? And at what moment would you have endured another examining your principles and proving that they were unsound? What then am I to say to you? "Help me in this matter!" you cry. Ah, for that I have no rule! And neither did you, if that was your object, come to me as a philosopher, but as you might have gone to a herb-seller or a cobbler.—"What do philosophers have rules for, then?"—Why, that whatever may betide, our ruling faculty may be as Nature would have it, and so remain. Think you this a small matter? Not so! but the greatest thing there is. Well, does it need but a short time? Can it be grasped by a passer-by?—grasp it, if you can!

Then you will say, "Yes, I met Epictetus!"

Aye, just as you might a statue or a monument. You saw me! and that is all. But a man who meets a man is one who learns the other's mind, and lets him see his in turn. Learn my mind—show me yours; and then go and say that you met me. Let us try each other; if I have any wrong principle, rid me of it; if you have, out with it. That is what meeting a philosopher means. Not so, you think; this is only a flying visit; while we are hiring the ship, we can see Epictetus too! Let us see what he has to say. Then on leaving you cry, "Out on Epictetus for a worthless fellow, provincial and barbarous of speech!" What else indeed did you come to judge of?

XCIV

Whether you will or no, you are poorer than I!
"What then do I lack?"
What you have not: Constancy of mind, such as Nature would have it be: Tranquillity. Patron or no patron, what care I? but you do care. I am richer than you: I am not racked with anxiety as to what Cæsar may think of me; I flatter none on that account. This is what I have, instead of vessels of gold and silver! your vessels may be of gold, but your reason, your principles, your accepted

views, your inclinations, your desires are of earthenware.

XCV

To you, all you have seems small: to me, all I have seems great. Your desire is insatiable, mine is satisfied. See children thrusting their hands into a narrow-necked jar, and striving to pull out the nuts and figs it contains: if they fill the hand, they cannot pull it out again, and then they fall to tears.—"Let go a few of them, and then you can draw out the rest!"—You, too, let your desire go! covet not many things, and you will obtain.

XCVI

Pittacus wronged by one whom he had it in his power to punish, let him go free, saying, Forgiveness is better than revenge. The one shows native gentleness, the other savagery.

XCVII

"My brother ought not to have treated me thus."
True: but he must see to that. However he may treat me, I must deal rightly by him. This is what lies with me, what none can hinder.

XCVIII

Nevertheless a man should also be prepared to be sufficient

unto himself—to dwell with himself alone, even as God dwells with Himself alone, shares His repose with none, and considers the nature of His own administration, intent upon such thoughts as are meet unto Himself. So should we also be able to converse with ourselves, to need none else beside, to sigh for no distraction, to bend our thoughts upon the Divine Administration, and how we stand related to all else; to observe how human accidents touched us of old, and how they touch us now; what things they are that still have power to hurt us, and how they may be cured or removed; to perfect what needs perfecting as Reason would direct.

XCIX

If a man has frequent intercourse with others, either in the way of conversation, entertainment, or simple familiarity, he must either become like them, or change them to his own fashion. A live coal placed next a dead one will either kindle that or be quenched by it. Such being the risk, it is well to be cautious in admitting intimacies of this sort, remembering that one cannot rub shoulders with a soot-stained man without sharing the soot oneself. What will you do, supposing the talk turns on gladiators, or horses, or prize-fighters, or (what is worse) on persons, condemning this and that, approving the other? Or suppose a man sneers and jeers or shows a malignant temper? Has any among us the skill of the lute-player, who knows at the first touch which strings are out of tune and sets the instrument right: has any of you such power as Socrates had, in all his intercourse with men, of winning them over to his own convictions? Nay, but you must needs be swayed hither and thither by the uninstructed. How comes it then that they prove so much stronger than you? Because they speak from the fulness of the heart—their low, corrupt views are their real convictions: whereas your fine sentiments are but from the lips, outwards; that is why they are so nerveless and dead. It turns one's stomach to listen to your exhortations, and hear of your miserable Virtue, that you prate of up and down. Thus it is that the Vulgar prove too strong for you.

Everywhere strength, everywhere victory waits your conviction!

C

In general, any methods of discipline applied to the body which tend to modify its desires or repulsions, are good—for ascetic ends. But if done for display, they betray at once a man who keeps an eye on outward show; who has an ulterior purpose, and is looking for spectators to shout, "Oh what a great man!" This is why Apollonius so well said: "If you are bent upon a little private discipline, wait till you are choking with heat some day—then take a mouthful of cold water, and spit it out again, and tell no man!"

CI

Study how to give as one that is sick: that thou mayest hereafter give as one that is whole. Fast; drink water only; abstain altogether from desire, that thou mayest hereafter conform thy desire to Reason.

CII

Thou wouldst do good unto men? then show them by thine own example what kind of men philosophy can make, and cease from foolish trifling. Eating, do good to them that eat with thee; drinking, to them that drink with thee; yield unto all, give way, and bear with them. Thus shalt thou do them good: but vent not upon them thine own evil humour!

CIII

Even as bad actors cannot sing alone, but only in chorus: so some cannot walk alone.

Man, if thou art aught, strive to walk alone and hold converse with thyself, instead of skulking in the chorus! at length think; look around thee; bestir thyself, that thou mayest know who thou art!

CIV

You would fain be victor at the Olympic games, you say. Yes, but weigh the conditions, weigh the consequences; then and then only, lay to your hand—if it be for your profit. You must live by rule, submit to diet, abstain from dainty meats, exercise your body perforce at stated hours, in heat or in cold; drink no cold water, nor, it may be, wine. In a word, you must surrender yourself wholly to your trainer, as though to a physician.

Then in the hour of contest, you will have to delve the ground, it may chance dislocate an arm, sprain an ankle, gulp down abundance of yellow sand, be scourge with the whip—and with all this sometimes lose the victory. Count the cost—and then, if your desire still holds, try the wrestler's life. Else let me tell you that you will be behaving like a pack of children playing now at wrestlers, now at gladiators; presently falling to trumpeting and anon to stage-playing, when the fancy takes them for what they have seen. And you are even the same: wrestler, gladiator, philosopher, orator all by turns and none of them with your whole soul. Like an ape, you mimic what you see, to one thing constant never; the thing that is familiar charms no more. This is because you never undertook aught with due consideration, nor after strictly testing and viewing it from every side; no, your choice was thoughtless; the glow of your desire had waxed cold . . . .

Friend, bethink you first what it is you would do, and then what your own nature is able to bear. Would you be a wrestler, consider your shoulders, your thighs, your loins—not all men are formed to the same end. Think you to be a philosopher while acting as you do? think you go on thus eating, thus drinking, giving way in like manner to wrath and to displeasure? Nay, you must watch, you must labour; overcome certain desires; quit your familiar friends, submit to be despised by your slave, to be held in derision by them that meet you, to take the lower place in all things, in office, in positions of authority, in courts of law.

Weigh these things fully, and then, if you will, lay to your hand; if as the price of these things you would gain Freedom, Tranquillity, and passionless Serenity.

CV

He that hath no musical instruction is a child in Music; he that hath no letters is a child in Learning; he that is untaught is a child in Life.

CVI

Can any profit be derived from these men? Aye, from all.

"What, even from a reviler?"

Why, tell me what profit a wrestler gains from him who exercises him beforehand? The very greatest: he trains me in the practice of endurance, of controlling my temper, of gentle ways. You deny it. What, the man who lays hold of my neck, and disciplines loins and shoulders, does me good, . . . while he that trains me to keep my temper does me none? This is what it means, not knowing how to gain advantage from men! Is my neighbour bad? Bad to himself, but good to me: he brings my good temper, my gentleness into play. Is my father bad? Bad to himself, but good to me. This is the rod of Hermes; touch what you will with it, they say, and it becomes gold. Nay, but bring what you will and I will transmute it into Good. Bring sickness, bring death, bring poverty and reproach, bring trial for life—all these things through the rod of Hermes shall be turned to profit.

CVII

Till then these sound opinions have taken firm root in you, and you have gained a measure of strength for your security, I counsel you to be cautious in associating with the uninstructed. Else whatever impressions you receive upon the tablets of your mind in the School will day by day melt and disappear, like wax in the sun. Withdraw then somewhere far from the sun, while you have these waxen sentiments.

CVIII

We must approach this matter in a different way; it is great and mystical: it is no common thing; nor given to every man. Wisdom alone, it may be, will not suffice for the care of youth: a man needs also a certain measure of readiness—an aptitude for the office; aye, and certain bodily qualities; and above all, to be counselled of God Himself to undertake this post; even as He counselled Socrates to fill the post of one who confutes error, assigning to Diogenes the royal office of high reproof, and to Zeno that of positive instruction. Whereas you would fain set up for a physician provided with nothing but drugs! Where and how they should be applied you neither know nor care.

CIX

If what charms you is nothing but abstract principles, sit down and turn them over quietly in your mind: but never dub yourself a Philosopher, nor suffer others to call you so. Say rather: He is in error; for my desires, my impulses are unaltered. I give in my adhesion to what I did before; nor has my mode of dealing with the things of sense undergone any change.

CX

When a friend inclined to Cynic views asked Epictetus, what sort of person a true Cynic should be, requesting a general sketch of the system, he answered:—"We will consider that at leisure. At present I content myself with saying this much: If a man put his hand to so weighty a matter without God, the wrath of God abides upon him. That which he covets will but bring upon him public shame. Not even on finding himself in a well-ordered house does a man step forward and say to himself, I must be master here! Else the lord of that house takes notice of it, and, seeing him insolently giving orders, drags him forth and chastises him. So it is also in this great City, the World. Here also is there a Lord of the House, who orders all thing:—

> "Thou are the Sun! in thine orbit thou hast
> power to make the year and the seasons;
> to bid the fruits of the earth to grow
> and increase, the winds arise and fall;
> thou canst in due measure cherish with
> thy warmth the frames of men; go make
> thy circuit, and thus minister unto all
> from the greatest to the least! . . ."

"Thou canst lead a host against Troy; be Agamemnon!"

"Thou canst meet Hector in single combat; be Achilles!"

"But had Thersites stepped forward and claimed the chief command, he had been met with a refusal, or obtained it only to his own shame and confusion of face, before a cloud of witnesses."

CXI

Others may fence themselves with walls and houses, when they do such deeds as these, and wrap themselves in darkness—aye, they have many a device to hide themselves. Another may shut his door and station one before his chamber to say, if any comes, He has gone forth! he is not at leisure! But the true Cynic will have none of these things; instead of them, he must wrap himself in Modesty: else he will but bring himself to shame, naked and under the open sky. That is his house; that is his door; that is the slave that guards his chamber; that is his darkness!

CXII

Death? let it come when it will, whether it smite but a part of the whole: Fly, you tell me—fly! But whither shall I fly? Can any man cast me beyond the limits of the World? It may not be! And whithersoever I go, there shall I still find Sun, Moon, and Stars; there I shall find dreams, and omens, and converse with the Gods!

CXIII

Furthermore the true Cynic must know that he is sent as a Messenger from God to men, to show unto them that as touching good and evil they are in error; looking for these where they are not to be found, nor ever bethinking themselves where they are. And like Diogenes when brought before Philip after the battle of Chaeronea, the Cynic must remember that he is a Spy. For a Spy he really is—to bring back word what things are on Man's side, and what against him. And when he had diligently observed all, he must come back with a true report, not terrified into announcing them to be foes that are no foes, nor otherwise perturbed or confounded by the things of sense.

CXIV

How can it be that one who hath nothing, neither raiment, nor house, nor home, nor bodily tendance, nor servant, nor city, should yet live tranquil and contented? Behold God hath sent you a man to show you in act and deed that it may be so. Behold me! I have neither house nor possessions nor servants: the ground is my couch; I have no wife, no children, no shelter—nothing but earth and sky, and one poor cloak. And what lack I yet? am I not untouched by sorrow, by fear? am I not free? ... when have I laid anything to the charge of God or Man? when have I accused any? hath any of you seen me with a sorrowful countenance? And in what wise treat I those of whom you stand in fear and awe? Is it not as slaves? Who when he seeth me doth not think that he beholdeth his Master and his King?

CXV

Give thyself more diligently to reflection: know thyself: take counsel with the Godhead: without God put thine hand unto nothing!

CXVI

"But to marry and to rear offspring," said the young man, "will the Cynic hold himself bound to undertake this as a chief duty?"

Grant me a republic of wise men, answered Epictetus, and

perhaps none will lightly take the Cynic life upon him. For on whose account should he embrace that method of life? Suppose however that he does, there will then be nothing to hinder his marrying and rearing offspring. For his wife will be even such another as himself, and likewise her father; and in like manner will his children be brought up.

But in the present condition of things, which resembles an Army in battle array, ought not the Cynic to be free from all distraction and given wholly to the service of God, so that he can go in and out among men, neither fettered by the duties nor entangled by the relations of common life? For if he transgress them, he will forfeit the character of a good man and true; whereas if he observe them, there is an end to him as the Messenger, the Spy, the Herald of the Gods!

CXVII

Ask me if you choose if a Cynic shall engage in the administration of the State. O fool, seek you a nobler administration that that in which he is engaged? Ask you if a man shall come forward in the Athenian assembly and talk about revenue and supplies, when his business is to converse with all men, Athenians, Corinthians, and Romans alike, not about supplies, not about revenue, nor yet peace and war, but about Happiness and Misery, Prosperity and Adversity, Slavery and Freedom?

Ask you whether a man shall engage in the administration of the State who has engaged in such an Administration as this? Ask me too if he shall govern; and again I will answer, Fool, what greater government shall he hold than he holds already?

CXVIII

Such a man needs also to have a certain habit of body. If he appears consumptive, thin and pale, his testimony has no longer the same authority. He must not only prove to the unlearned by showing them what his Soul is that it is possible to be a good man apart from all that they admire; but he must also show them, by his body, that a plain and simple manner of life under the open sky does no harm to the body either. "See, I am proof of this! and my body also." As Diogenes used to do, who went about fresh of look and by the very appearance of his body drew men's eyes. But if a Cynic is an object of pity, he seems a mere beggar; all turn away, all are offended at him. Nor should he be slovenly of look, so as not to scare men from him in this way either; on the contrary, his very roughness should be clean and attractive.

CXIX

Kings and tyrants have armed guards wherewith to chastise certain persons, though they themselves be evil. But to the Cynic conscience gives this power—not arms and guards. When he knows that he has watched and laboured on behalf of mankind: that sleep hath found him pure, and left him purer still: that his thoughts have been the thought of a Friend of the Gods—of a servant, yet one that hath a part in the government of the Supreme God: that the words are ever on his lips:—
Lead me, O God, and thou, O Destiny!
as well as these:—
If this be God's will, so let it be!
Why should he not speak boldly unto his own brethren, unto his children—in a word, unto all that are akin to him!

CXX

Does a Philosopher apply to people to come and hear him? does he not rather, of his own nature, attract those that will be benefited by him—like the sun that warms, the food that sustains them? What Physician applies to men to come and be healed? (Though indeed I hear that the Physicians at Rome do nowadays apply for patients—in my time they were applied to.) I apply to you to come and hear that you are in evil case; that what deserves your attention most is the last thing to gain it; that you know not good from evil, and are in short a hapless wretch; a fine way to apply! though unless the words of the Philosopher affect you thus, speaker and speech are alike dead.

CXXI

A Philosopher's school is a Surgery: pain, not pleasure, you should have felt therein. For on entering none of you is whole. One has a shoulder out of joint, another an abscess: a third suffers from an issue, a fourth from pains in the head. And am I then to sit down and treat you to pretty sentiments and empty flourishes, so that you may applaud me and depart, with neither shoulder, nor head, nor issue, nor abscess a whit the better for your visit? Is it then for this that young men are to quit their homes, and leave parents, friends, kinsmen and substance to mouth out Bravo to your empty phrases!

CXXII

If any be unhappy, let him remember that he is unhappy by reason of himself alone. For God hath made all men to enjoy felicity and constancy of good.

CXXIII

Shall we never wean ourselves—shall we never heed the teachings of Philosophy (unless perchance they have been sounding in our ears like an enchanter's drone):—

This World is one great City, and one is the substance whereof it is fashioned: a certain period indeed there needs must be, while these give place to those; some must perish for others to succeed; some move and some abide: yet all is full of friends—first God, then Men, whom Nature hath bound by ties of kindred each to each.

CXXIV

Nor did the hero weep and lament at leaving his children orphans. For he knew that no man is an orphan, but it is the Father that careth for all continually and for evermore. Not by mere report had he heard that the Supreme God is the Father of men: seeing that he called Him Father believing Him so to be, and in all that he did had ever his eyes fixed upon Him. Wherefore in whatsoever place he was, there is was given him to live happily.

CXXV

Know you not that the thing is a warfare? one man's duty is to mount guard, another must go out to reconnoitre, a third to battle; all cannot be in one place, nor would it even be expedient. But you, instead of executing you Commander's orders, complain if aught harsher than usual is enjoined; not understanding to what condition you are bringing the army, so far as in you lies. If all were to follow your example, none would dig a trench, none would cast a rampart around the camp, none would keep watch, or expose himself to danger; but all turn out useless for the service of war. . . . Thus it is here also. Every life is a warfare, and that long and various. You must fulfil a soldier's duty, and obey each order at your commander's nod: aye, if it be possible, divine what he would have done; for between that Command and this, there is no comparison, either in might or in excellence.

CXXVI

Have you again forgotten? Know you not that a good man does nothing for appearance' sake, but for the sake of having done right? . . .

"Is there no reward then?"

Reward! do you seek any greater reward for a good man than doing what is right and just? Yet at the Great Games you look for nothing else; there the victor's crown you deem enough. Seems it to you so small a thing and worthless, to be a good man, and happy therein?

CXXVII

It befits thee not to be unhappy by reason of any, but rather to be happy by reason of all men, and especially by reason of God, who formed us to this end.

CXXVIII

What, did Diogenes love no man, he that was so gentle, so true a friend to men as cheerfully to endure such bodily hardships for the common weal of all mankind? But how loved he them? As behoved a minister of the Supreme God, alike caring for men and subject unto God.

CXXIX

I am by Nature made for my own good; not for my own evil.

CXXX

Remind thyself that he whom thou lovest is mortal—that what thou lovest is not thine own; it is given thee for the present, not irrevocably nor for ever, but even as a fig or a bunch of grapes at the appointed season of the year. . . .

"But these are words of evil omen.". . .

What, callest thou aught of evil omen save that which signifies some evil thing? Cowardice is a word of evil omen, if thou wilt, and meanness of spirit, and lamentation and mourning, and shamelessness. . . .

But do not, I pray thee, call of evil omen a word that is significant of any natural thing:—as well call of evil omen the reaping of the corn; for that means the destruction of the ears, though not of the World!—as well say that the fall of the leaf is of evil omen; that the dried fig should take the place of the green; that raisins should be made from grapes. All these are changes from a former state into another; not destruction, but an ordered economy, a fixed administration. Such is leaving home, a change of small account; such is Death, a greater change, from what now is, not to what is not, but to what is not now.

"Shall I then no longer be?"

Not so; thou wilt be; but something different, of which the World now hath need. For thou too wert born not when thou chosest, but when the World had need of thee.

CXXXI

Wherefore a good man and true, bearing in mind who he is and whence he came and from whom he sprang, cares only how he may fill his post with due discipline and obedience to God.

Wilt thou that I continue to live? Then will I live, as one that is free and noble, as Thou wouldst have me. For Thou hast made me free from hindrance in what appertaineth unto me. But hast Thou no further need of me? I thank Thee! Up to this hour have I stayed for Thy sake and none other's: and now in obedience to Thee I depart.

"How dost thou depart?"

Again I say, as Thou wouldst have me; as one that is free, as Thy servant, as one whose ear is open unto what Thou dost enjoin, what Thou dost forbid.

CXXXII

Whatsoever place or post Thou assignest me, sooner will I die a thousand deaths, as Socrates said, than desert it. And where wilt Thou have me to be? At Rome or Athens? At Thebes or on a desert island? Only remember me there! Shouldst Thou send me where man cannot live as Nature would have him, I will depart, not in disobedience to Thee, but as though Thou wert sounding the signal for my retreat: I am not deserting Thee—far be that from me! I only perceive that thou needest me no longer.

CXXXIII

If you are in Gyaros, do not let your mind dwell upon life at Rome, and all the pleasures it offered to you when living there, and all that would attend your return. Rather be intent on this—how he that lives in Gyaros may live in Gyaros like a man of spirit. And if you are at Rome, do not let your mind dwell upon the life at Athens, but study only how to live at Rome.

Finally, in the room of all other pleasures put this—the pleasure which springs from conscious obedience to God.

CXXXIV

To a good man there is no evil, either in life or death. And if God supply not food, has He not, as a wise Commander, sounded the signal for retreat and nothing more? I obey, I follow—speaking good of my Commander, and praising His acts. For at His good pleasure I came; and I depart when it pleases Him; and while I was yet alive that was my work, to sing praises unto God!

CXXXV

Reflect that the chief source of all evils to Man, and of baseness and cowardice, is not death, but the fear of death.
Against this fear then, I pray you, harden yourself; to this let all your reasonings, your exercises, your reading tend. Then shall you know that thus alone are men set free.

CXXXVI

He is free who lives as he wishes to live; to whom none can do violence, none hinder or compel; whose impulses are unimpeded, whose desires are attain their purpose, who falls not into what he would avoid. Who then would live in error?—None. Who would live deceived and prone to fall, unjust, intemperate, in abject whining at his lot?—None. Then doth no wicked man live as he would, and therefore neither is he free.

CXXXVII

Thus do the more cautious of travellers act. The road is said to be beset by robbers. The traveller will not venture alone, but awaits the companionship on the road of an ambassador, a quaestor or a proconsul. To him he attaches himself and thus passes by in safety. So doth the wise man in the world. Many are the companies of robbers and tyrants, many the storms, the straits, the losses of all a man holds dearest. Whither shall he fall for refuge—how shall he pass by unassailed? What companion on the road shall he await for protection? Such and such a wealthy man, of consular rank? And how shall I be profited, if he is stripped and falls to lamentation and weeping? And how if my fellow-traveller himself turns upon me and robs me? What am I to do? I will become a friend of Cæsar's! in his train none will do me wrong! In the first place—O the indignities I must endure to win distinction! O the multitude of hands there will be to rob me! And if I succeed, Cæsar too is but a mortal. While should it come to pass that I offend him, whither shall I flee from his presence? To the wilderness? And may not fever await me there? What then is to be done? Cannot a fellow-traveller be found that is honest and loyal, strong and secure against surprise? Thus doth the wise man reason, considering that if he would pass through in safety, he must attach himself unto God.

CXXXVIII

"How understandest thou attach himself to God?"

That what God wills, he should will also; that what God wills not, neither should he will.

"How then may this come to pass?"

By considering the movements of God, and His administration.

CXXXIX

And dost thou that hast received all from another's hands, repine and blame the Giver, if He takes anything from thee? Why, who art thou, and to what end comest thou here? was it not He that made the Light manifest unto thee, that gave thee fellow-workers, and senses, and the power to reason? And how brought He thee into the world? Was it not as one born to die; as one bound to live out his earthly life in some small tabernacle of flesh; to behold His administration, and for a little while share with Him in the mighty march of this great Festival Procession? Now therefore that thou hast beheld, while it was permitted thee, the Solemn Feast and Assembly, wilt thou not cheerfully depart, when He summons thee forth, with adoration and thanksgiving for what thou hast seen and heard?—"Nay, but I would fain have stayed longer at the Festival."—Ah, so would the mystics fain have the rites prolonged; so perchance would the crowd at the Great Games fain behold more wrestlers still. But the Solemn Assembly is over! Come forth, depart with thanksgiving and modesty—give place to others that must come into being even as thyself.

CXL

Why art thou thus insatiable? why thus unreasonable? why encumber the world?—"Aye, but I fain would have my wife and children with me too."—What, are they then thine, and not His that gave them—His that made thee? Give up then that which is not thine own: yield it to One who is better than thou. "Nay, but why did He bring one into the world on these conditions?"—If it suits thee not, depart! He hath no need of a spectator who finds fault with his lot! Them that will take part in the Feast he needeth—that will lift their voices with the rest that men may applaud the more, and exalt the Great Assembly in hymns and songs of praise. But the wretched and the fearful He will not be displeased to see absent from it: for when they were present, they did not behave as at a Feast, nor fulfil their proper office; but moaned as though in pain, and found fault with their fate, their fortune and their companions; insensible to what had fallen to their lot, insensible to the powers they had received for a very different purpose—the powers of Magnanimity, Nobility of Heart, of Fortitude, or Freedom!

CXLI

Art thou then free? a man may say. So help me heaven, I long and pray for freedom! But I cannot look my masters boldly in the face; I still value the poor body; I still set much store on its preservation whole and sound.

But I can point thee out a free man, that thou mayest be no more in search of an example. Diogenes was free. How so? Not because he was of free parentage (for that, indeed, was not the case), but because he was himself free. He had cast away every handle whereby slavery might lay hold of him to enslave him, nor was it possible for any to approach and take hold of him to enslave him. All things sat loose upon him—all things were to him attached by but slender ties. Hadst thou seized upon his possessions, he would rather have let them go than have followed thee for them—aye, had it been even a limb, or mayhap his whole body; and in like manner, relatives, friends, and country. For he knew whence they came—from whose hands and on what terms he had received them. His true forefathers, the Gods, his true Country, he never would have abandoned; nor would he have yielded to any man in obedience and submission to the one nor in cheerfully dying for the other. For he was ever mindful that everything that comes to pass has its source and origin there; being indeed brought about for the weal of that his true Country, and directed by Him in whose governance it is.

CXLII

Ponder on this—on these convictions, on these words: fix

thine eyes on these examples, if thou wouldst be free, if thou hast thine heart set upon the matter according to its worth. And what marvel if thou purchase so great a thing at so great and high a price? For the sake of this that men deem liberty, some hang themselves, others cast themselves down from the rock; aye, time has been when whole cities came utterly to an end: while for the sake of Freedom that is true, and sure, and unassailable, dost thou grudge to God what He gave, when He claims it? Wilt thou not study, as Plato saith, to endure, not death alone, but torture, exile, stripes—in a word, to render up all that is not thine own? Else thou wilt be a slave amid slaves, wert thou ten thousand times a consul; aye, not a whit the less, though thou climb the Palace steps. And thou shalt know how true the saying of Cleanthes, that though the words of philosophers may run counter to the opinions of the world, yet have they reason on their side.

CXLIII

Asked how a man should best grieve his enemy, Epictetus replied, "By setting himself to live the noblest life himself."

CXLIV

I am free, I am a friend of God, ready to render Him willing obedience. Of all else I may set store by nothing—neither by mine own body, nor possessions, nor office, nor good report, nor, in a word, aught else beside. For it is not His Will, that I should so set store by these things. Had it been His pleasure, He would have placed my Good therein. But now He hath not done so: therefore I cannot transgress one jot of His commands. In everything hold fast to that which is thy Good—but to all else (as far as is given thee) within the measure of Reason only, contented with this alone. Else thou wilt meet with failure, ill success, let and hindrance. These are the Laws ordained of God—these are His Edicts; these a man should expound and interpret; to these submit himself, not to the laws of Masurius and Cassius.

CXLV

Remember that not the love of power and wealth sets us under the heel of others, but even the love of tranquillity, of leisure, of change of scene—of learning in general, it matters not what the outward thing may be—to set store by it is to place thyself in subjection to another. Where is the difference then between desiring to be a Senator, and desiring not to be one: between thirsting for office and thirsting to be quit of it? Where is the difference between crying, Woe is me, I know not what to do, bound hand and foot as I am to my books so that I cannot stir! and crying, Woe is me, I have not time to read! As though a book were not as much an outward thing and independent of the will, as office and power and the receptions of the great.

Or what reason hast thou (tell me) for desiring to read? For if thou aim at nothing beyond the mere delight of it, or gaining some scrap of knowledge, thou art but a poor, spiritless knave. But if thou desirest to study to its proper end, what else is this than a life that flows on tranquil and serene? And if thy reading secures thee not serenity, what profits it?—"Nay, but it doth secure it," quoth he, "and that is why I repine at being deprived of it."—And what serenity is this that lies at the mercy of every passer-by? I say not at the mercy of the Emperor or Emperor's favorite, but such as trembles at a raven's croak and piper's din, a fever's touch or a thousand things of like sort! Whereas the life serene has no more certain mark than this, that it ever moves with constant unimpeded flow.

CXLVI

If thou hast put malice and evil speaking from thee, altogether, or in some degree: if thou hast put away from thee rashness, foulness of tongue, intemperance, sluggishness: if thou art not moved by what once moved thee, or in like manner as thou once wert moved—then thou mayest celebrate a daily festival, to-day because thou hast done well in this manner, to-morrow in that. How much greater cause is here for offering sacrifice, than if a man should become Consul or Prefect?

CXLVII

These things hast thou from thyself and from the Gods: only remember who it is that giveth them—to whom and for what purpose they were given. Feeding thy soul on thoughts like these, dost thou debate in what place happiness awaits thee? in what place thou shalt do God's pleasure? Are not the Gods nigh unto all places alike; see they not alike what everywhere comes to pass?

CXLVIII

To each man God hath granted this inward freedom. These are the principles that in a house create love, in a city concord, among nations peace, teaching a man gratitude towards God and cheerful confidence, wherever he may be, in dealing with outward things that he knows are neither his nor worth striving after.

CXLIX

If you seek Truth, you will not seek to gain a victory by every possible means; and when you have found Truth, you need not fear being defeated.

CL

What foolish talk is this? how can I any longer lay claim to right principles, if I am not content with being what I am, but am all aflutter about what I am supposed to be?

CLI

God hath made all things in the world, nay, the world itself, free from hindrance and perfect, and its parts for the use of the whole. No other creature is capable of comprehending His administration thereof; but the reasonable being Man possesses faculties for the consideration of all these things—not only that he is himself a part, but what part he is, and how it is meet that the parts should give place to the whole. Nor is this all. Being naturally constituted noble, magnanimous, and free, he sees that the things which surround him are of two kinds. Some are free from hindrance and in the power of the will. Other are subject to hindrance, and depend on the will of other men. If then he place his own good, his own best interest, only in that which is free from hindrance and in his power, he will be free, tranquil, happy, unharmed, noble-hearted, and pious; giving thanks to all things unto God, finding fault with nothing that comes to pass, laying no charge against anything. Whereas if he place his good in outward things, depending not on the will, he must perforce be subject to hindrance and restraint, the slave of those that have power over the things he desires and fears; he must perforce be impious, as deeming himself injured at the hands of God; he must be unjust, as ever prone to claim more than his due; he must perforce be of a mean and abject spirit.

CLII

Whom then shall I fear? the lords of the Bedchamber, lest they should shut me out? If they find me desirous of entering in, let them shut me out, if they will.

"Then why comest thou to the door?"

Because I think it meet and right, so long as the Play lasts, to take part therein.

"In what sense art thou then shut out?"

Because, unless I am admitted, it is not my will to enter: on the contrary, my will is simply that which comes to pass. For I esteem what God wills better than what I will. To Him will I cleave as His minister and attendant; having the same movements, the same desires, in a word the same Will as He. There is no such thing as being shut out for me, but only for them that would force their way in.

CLIII

But what says Socrates?—"One man finds pleasure in improving his land, another his horses. My pleasure lies in seeing that I myself grow better day by day."

CLIV

The dress is suited to the craft; the craftsman takes his name from the craft, not from the dress. For this reason Euphrates was right in saying, "I long endeavoured to conceal my following the philosophic life; and this profited me much. In the first place, I knew that what I did aright, I did not for the sake of lookers-on, but for my own. I ate aright—unto myself; I kept the even tenor of my walk, my glance composed and serene—all unto myself and unto God. Then as I fought alone, I was alone in peril. If I did anything amiss or shameful, the cause of Philosophy was not in me endangered; nor did I wrong the multitude by transgressing as a professed philosopher. Wherefore those that knew not my purpose marvelled how it came about, that whilst all my life and conversation was passed with philosophers without exception, I was yet none myself. And what harm that the philosopher should be known by his acts, instead of mere outward signs and symbols?"

CLV

First study to conceal what thou art; seek wisdom a little while unto thyself. Thus grows the fruit; first, the seed must be buried in the earth for a little space; there it must be hid and slowly grow, that it may reach maturity. But if it produce the ear before the jointed stalk, it is imperfect—a thing from the garden of Adonis. Such a sorry growth art thou; thou hast blossomed too soon: the winter cold will wither thee away!

CLVI

First of all, condemn the life thou art now leading: but when thou hast condemned it, do not despair of thyself—be not like them of mean spirit, who once they have yielded, abandon themselves entirely and as it were allow the torrent to sweep them away. No; learn what the wrestling masters do. Has the boy fallen? "Rise," they say, "wrestle again, till thy strength come to thee." Even thus should it be with thee. For know that there is nothing more tractable than the human soul. It needs but to will, and the thing is done; the soul is set upon the right path: as on the contrary it needs but to nod over the task, and all is lost. For ruin and recovery alike are from within.

CLVII

It is the critical moment that shows the man. So when the crisis is upon you, remember that God, like a trainer of wrestlers, has matched you with a rough and stalwart antagonist.—"To what end?" you ask. That you may prove the victor at the Great Games. Yet without toil and sweat this may not be!

CLVIII

If thou wouldst make progress, be content to seem foolish and void of understanding with respect to outward things. Care not to be thought to know anything. If any should make account of thee, distrust thyself.

CLIX

Remember that in life thou shouldst order thy conduct as at a banquet. Has any dish that is being served reached thee? Stretch forth thy hand and help thyself modestly. Doth it pass thee by? Seek not to detain it. Has it not yet come? Send not forth thy desire to meet it, but wait until it reaches thee. Deal thus with children, thus with wife; thus with office, thus with wealth—and one day thou wilt be meet to share the Banquets of the Gods. But if thou dost not so much as touch that which is placed before thee, but despisest it, then shalt thou not only share the Banquets of the Gods, but their Empire also.

CLX

Remember that thou art an actor in a play, and of such sort as the Author chooses, whether long or short. If it be his good pleasure to assign thee the part of a beggar, a ruler, or a simple citizen, thine it is to play it fitly. For thy business is to act the part assigned thee, well: to choose it, is another's.

CLXI

Keep death and exile daily before thine eyes, with all else that men deem terrible, but more especially Death. Then wilt thou never think a mean though, nor covet anything beyond measure.

CLXII

As a mark is not set up in order to be missed, so neither is such a thing as natural evil produced in the World.

CLXIII

Piety toward the Gods, to be sure, consists chiefly in thinking rightly concerning them—that they are, and that they govern the Universe with goodness and justice; and that thou thyself art appointed to obey them, and to submit under all circumstances that arise; acquiescing cheerfully in whatever may happen, sure it is brought to pass and accomplished by the most Perfect Understanding. Thus thou wilt never find fault with the Gods, nor charge them with neglecting thee.

CLXIV

Lose no time in setting before you a certain stamp of character and behaviour both when by yourself and in company with others. Let silence be your general rule; or say only what is necessary and in few words. We shall, however, when occasion demands, enter into discourse sparingly. avoiding common topics as gladiators, horse-races, athletes; and the perpetual talk about food and drink. Above all avoid speaking of persons, either in way of praise or blame, or comparison.

If you can, win over the conversation of your company to what it should be by your own. But if you find yourself cut off without escape among strangers and aliens, be silent.

CLXV

Laughter should not be much, nor frequent, nor unrestrained.

CLXVI

Refuse altogether to take an oath if you can, if not, as far as may be.

CLXVII

Banquets of the unlearned and of them that are without, avoid. But if you have occasion to take part in them, let not your attention be relaxed for a moment, lest you slip after all into evil ways. For you may rest assured that be a man ever so pure himself, he cannot escape defilement if his associates are impure.

CLXVIII

Take what relates to the body as far as the bare use warrants—as meat, drink, raiment, house and servants. But all that makes for show and luxury reject.

CLXIX

If you are told that such an one speaks ill of you, make no defence against what was said, but answer, He surely knew not my other faults, else he would not have mentioned these only!

CLXX

When you visit any of those in power, bethink yourself that you will not find him in: that you may not be admitted: that the door may be shut in your face: that he may not concern himself about you. If with all this, it is your duty to go, bear what happens, and never say to yourself, It was not worth the trouble! For that would smack of the foolish and unlearned who suffer outward things to touch them.

CLXXI

In company avoid frequent and undue talk about your own actions and dangers. However pleasant it may be to you to enlarge upon the risks you have run, others may not find such pleasure in listening to your adventures. Avoid provoking laughter also: it is a habit from which one easily slides into the ways of the foolish, and apt to diminish the respect which your neighbors feel for you. To border on coarse talk is also dangerous. On such occasions, if a convenient opportunity offer, rebuke the speaker. If not, at least by relapsing into silence, colouring, and looking annoyed, show that you are displeased with the subject.

CLXXII

When you have decided that a thing ought to be done, and are doing it, never shun being seen doing it, even though the multitude should be likely to judge the matter amiss. For if you are not acting rightly, shun the act itself; if rightly, however, why fear misplaced censure?

CLXXIII

It stamps a man of mean capacity to spend much time on the things of the body, as to be long over bodily exercises, long over eating, long over drinking, long over other bodily functions. Rather should these things take the second place, while all your care is directed to the understanding.

CLXXIV

Everything has two handles, one by which it may be borne, the other by which it may not. If your brother sin against you lay not hold of it by the handle of injustice, for by that it may not be borne: but rather by this, that he is your brother, the comrade of your youth; and thus you will lay hold on it so that it may be borne.

CLXXV

Never call yourself a Philosopher nor talk much among the unlearned about Principles, but do that which follows from them. Thus at a banquet, do not discuss how people ought to eat; but eat as you ought. Remember that Socrates thus entirely avoided ostentation. Men would come to him desiring to be recommended to philosophers, and he would conduct them thither himself—so well did he bear being overlooked. Accordingly if any talk concerning principles should arise among the unlearned, be you for the most part silent. For you run great risk of spewing up what you have ill digested. And when a man tells you that you know nothing and you are not nettled at it, then you may be sure that you have begun the work.

CLXXVI

When you have brought yourself to supply the needs of the body at small cost, do not pique yourself on that, nor if you drink only water, keep saying on each occasion, I drink water! And if you ever want to practise endurance and toil, do so unto yourself and not unto others—do not embrace statues!

CLXXVII

When a man prides himself on being able to understand and interpret the writings of Chrysippus, say to yourself:—

If Chrysippus had not written obscurely, this fellow would have had nothing to be proud of. But what is it that I desire? To understand Nature, and to follow her! Accordingly I ask who is the Interpreter. On hearing that it is Chrysippus, I go to him. But it seems I do not understand what he wrote. So I seek one to interpret that. So far there is nothing to pride myself on. But when I have found my interpreter, what remains is to put in practice his instructions. This itself is the only thing to be proud of. But if I admire the interpretation and that alone, what else have I turned out but a mere commentator instead of a lover of wisdom?—except indeed that I happen to be interpreting Chrysippus instead of Homer. So when any one says to me, Prithee, read me Chrysippus, I am more inclined to blush, when I cannot show my deeds to be in harmony and accordance with his sayings.

CLXXVIII

At feasts, remember that you are entertaining two guests, body and soul. What you give to the body, you presently lose; what you give to the soul, you keep for ever.

CLXXIX

At meals, see to it that those who serve be not more in number than those who are served. It is absurd for a crowd of persons to be dancing attendance on half a dozen chairs.

CLXXX

It is best to share with your attendants what is going forward, both in the labour of preparation and in the enjoyment of the feast itself. If such a thing be difficult at the time, recollect that you who are not weary are being served by those that are; you who are eating and drinking by those who do neither; you who are talking by those who are silent; you who are at ease by those who are under constraint. Thus no sudden wrath will betray you into unreasonable conduct, nor will you behave harshly by irritating another.

CLXXXI

When Xanthippe was chiding Socrates for making scanty preparation for entertaining his friends, he answered:—"If they are friends of ours they will not care for that; if they are not, we shall care nothing for them!"

CLXXXII

Asked, Who is the rich man? Epictetus replied, "He who is content."

CLXXXIII

Favorinus tells us how Epictetus would also say that there were two faults far graver and fouler than any others—inability to bear, and inability to forbear, when we neither patiently bear the blows that must be borne, nor abstain from the things and the pleasures we ought to abstain from. "So," he went on, "if a man will only have these two words at heart, and heed them carefully by ruling and watching over himself, he will for the most part fall into no sin, and his life will be tranquil and serene." He meant the words [Greek: Anechou kai apechou]—"Bear and Forbear."

CLXXXIV

On all occasions these thoughts should be at hand:—
    Lead me, O God, and Thou, O Destiny
    Be what it may the goal appointed me,
    Bravely I'll follow; nay, and if I would not,
    I'd prove a coward, yet must follow still!
Again:
    Who to Necessity doth bow aright,
    Is learn'd in wisdom and the things of God.
Once more:—
    Crito, if this be God's will, so let it be. As for me,
    Anytus and Meletus can indeed put me to death, but injure me,
        never!

CLXXXV

We shall then be like Socrates, when we can indite hymns of praise to the Gods in prison.

CLXXXVI

It is hard to combine and unite these two qualities, the

carefulness of one who is affected by circumstances, and the intrepidity of one who heeds them not. But it is not impossible: else were happiness also impossible. We should act as we do in seafaring.

"What can I do?"—Choose the master, the crew, the day, the opportunity. Then comes a sudden storm. What matters it to me? my part has been fully done. The matter is in the hands of another—the Master of the ship. The ship is foundering. What then have I to do? I do the only thing that remains to me—to be drowned without fear, without a cry, without upbraiding God, but knowing that what has been born must likewise perish. For I am not Eternity, but a human being—a part of the whole, as an hour is part of the day. I must come like the hour, and like the hour must pass!

CLXXXVII

And now we are sending you to Rome to spy out the land; but none send a coward as such a spy, that, if he hear but a noise and see a shadow moving anywhere, loses his wits and comes flying to say, The enemy are upon us!

So if you go now, and come and tell us: "Everything at Rome is terrible: Death is terrible, Exile is terrible, Slander is terrible, Want is terrible; fly, comrades! the enemy are upon us!" we shall reply, Get you gone, and prophesy to yourself! we have but erred in sending such a spy as you. Diogenes, who was sent as a spy long before you, brought us back another report than this. He says that Death is no evil; for it need not even bring shame with it. He says that Fame is but the empty noise of madmen. And what report did this spy bring us of Pain, what of Pleasure, what of Want? That to be clothed in sackcloth is better than any purple robe; that sleeping on the bare ground is the softest couch; and in proof of each assertion he points to his own courage, constancy, and freedom; to his own healthy and muscular frame. "There is no enemy near," he cries, "all is perfect peace!"

CLXXXVIII

If a man has this peace—not the peace proclaimed by Cæsar (how indeed should he have it to proclaim?), nay, but the peace proclaimed by God through reason, will not that suffice him when alone, when he beholds and reflects:—Now can no evil happen unto me; for me there is no robber, for me no earthquake; all things are full of peace, full of tranquillity; neither highway nor city nor gathering of men, neither neighbor nor comrade can do me hurt. Another supplies my food, whose care it is; another my raiment; another hath given me perceptions of sense and primary conceptions. And when He supplies my necessities no more, it is that He is sounding the retreat, that He hath opened the door, and is saying to thee, Come!—Wither? To nought that thou needest fear, but to the friendly kindred elements whence thou didst spring. Whatsoever of fire is in thee, unto fire shall return; whatsoever of earth, unto earth; of spirit, unto spirit; of water, unto water. There is no Hades, no fabled rivers of Sighs, of Lamentation, or of Fire: but all things are full of Beings spiritual and divine. With thoughts like these, beholding the Sun, Moon, and Stars, enjoying earth and sea, a man is neither helpless nor alone!

CLXXXIX

What wouldst thou be found doing when overtaken by Death? If I might choose, I would be found doing some deed of true humanity, of wide import, beneficent and noble. But if I may not be found engaged in aught so lofty, let me hope at least for this—what none may hinder, what is surely in my power—that I may be found raising up in myself that which had fallen; learning to deal more wisely with the things of sense; working out my own tranquillity, and thus rendering that which is its due to every relation of life. . . .

If death surprise me thus employed, it is enough if I can

stretch forth my hands to God and say, "The faculties which I received at Thy hands for apprehending this thine Administration, I have not neglected. As far as in me lay, I have done Thee no dishonour. Behold how I have used the senses, the primary conceptions which Thous gavest me. Have I ever laid anything to Thy charge? Have I ever murmured at aught that came to pass, or wished it otherwise? Have I in anything transgressed the relations of life? For that Thou didst beget me, I thank Thee for that Thou hast given: for the time during which I have used the things that were Thine, it suffices me. Take them back and place them wherever Thou wilt! They were all Thine, and Thou gavest them me."—If a man depart thus minded, is it not enough? What life is fairer and more noble, what end happier than his?

(APPENDIX A)

Fragments Attributed to Epictetus

I

A life entangled with Fortune is like a torrent. It is turbulent and muddy; hard to pass and masterful of mood: noisy and of brief continuance.

II

The soul that companies with Virtue is like an ever-flowing source. It is a pure, clear, and wholesome draught; sweet, rich, and generous of its store; that injures not, neither destroys.

III

It is a shame that one who sweetens his drink with the gifts of the bee, should embitter God's gift Reason with vice.

IV

Crows pick out the eyes of the dead, when the dead have no longer need of them; but flatterers mar the soul of the living, and her eyes they blind.

V

Keep neither a blunt knife nor an ill-disciplined looseness of tongue.

VI

Nature hath given men one tongue but two ears, that we may hear from others twice as much as we speak.

VII

Do not give sentence in another tribunal till you have been yourself judged in the tribunal of Justice.

VIII

If is shameful for a Judge to be judged by others.

IX

Give me by all means the shorter and nobler life, instead of one that is longer but of less account!

X

Freedom is the name of virtue: Slavery, of vice. . . . None is a slave whose acts are free.

XI

Of pleasures, those which occur most rarely give the most delight.

XII

Exceed due measure, and the most delightful things become the least delightful.

XIII

The anger of an ape—the threat of a flatterer:—these deserve equal regard.

XIV

Chastise thy passions that they avenge not themselves upon thee.

XV

No man is free who is not master of himself.

XVI

A ship should not ride on a single anchor, nor life on a single hope.

XVII

Fortify thyself with contentment: that is an impregnable stronghold.

XVIII

No man who is a lover of money, of pleasure, of glory, is likewise a lover of Men; but only he that is a lover of whatsoever things are fair and good.

XIX

Think of God more often than thou breathest.

XX

Choose the life that is noblest, for custom can make it sweet to thee.

XXI

Let thy speech of God be renewed day by day, aye, rather than thy meat and drink.

XXII

Even as the Sun doth not wait for prayers and incantations to rise, but shines forth and is welcomed by all: so thou also wait not for clapping of hands and shouts and praise to do thy duty; nay, do good of thine own accord, and thou wilt be loved like the Sun.

XXIII

Let no man think that he is loved by any who loveth none.

XXIV

If thou rememberest that God standeth by to behold and visit all that thou doest; whether in the body or in the soul, thou surely wilt not err in any prayer or deed; and thou shalt have God to dwell with thee.

Note.—Schweighüser's great edition collects 181 fragments attributed to Epictetus, of which but a few are certainly genuine. Some (as xxi., xxiv., above) bear the stamp of Pythagorean origin; others, though changed in form, may well be based upon Epictetean sayings. Most have been preserved in the Anthology of John of Stobi (Stobæus), a Byzantine collector, of whom scarcely anything is known but that he probably wrote towards the end of the fifth century, and made his vast body of extracts from more than five hundred authors for his son's use. The best examination of the authenticity of the Fragments is Quaestiones Epicteteæ, by R. Asmus, 1888. The above selection includes some of doubtful origin but intrinsic interest.—Crossley.

THE HYMN OF CLEANTHES

Chiefest glory of deathless Gods, Almighty for ever,
Sovereign of Nature that rulest by law, what Name shall we give Thee?--
Blessed be Thou! for on Thee should call all things that are mortal.
For that we are Thine offspring; nay, all that in myriad motion
Lives for its day on the earth bears one impress--Thy likeness--upon it.
Wherefore my song is of Thee, and I hymn thy power for ever.

Lo, the vast orb of the Worlds, round the Earth evermore as it rolleth,
Feels Thee its Ruler and Guide, and owns Thy lordship rejoicing.
Aye, for Thy conquering hands have a servant of living fire--
Sharp is the bolt!--where it falls, Nature shrinks at the shock
and doth shudder.
Thus Thou directest the Word universal that pulses through all things,
Mingling its life with Lights that are great and Lights that are lesser,
E'en as beseemeth its birth, High King through ages unending.

Nought is done that is done without Thee in the earth or the waters
Or in the heights of heaven, save the deed of the fool and the sinner.
Thou canst make rough things smooth; at Thy voice, lo, jarring disorder
Moveth to music, and Love is born where hatred abounded.
Thus hast Thou fitted alike things good and things evil together,
That over all might reign one Reason, supreme and eternal;
Though thereunto the hearts of the wicked be hardened and heedless--
Woe unto them!--for while ever their hands are grasping at good things,
Blind are their eyes, yea, stopped are their ears to God's Law universal,

Calling through wise disobedience to live the life that is noble.
This they mark not, but heedless of right, turn each to his own way,
Here, a heart fired with ambition, in strife and straining unhallowed;
There, thrusting honour aside, fast set upon getting and gaining;
Others again given over to lusts and dissolute softness,
Working never God's Law, but that which warreth upon it.

Nay, but, O Giver of all things good, whose home is the dark cloud,
Thou that wieldesy Heaven's bolt, save men from their ignorance grievous;
Scatter its night from their souls, and grant them to come to that Wisdom
Wherewithal, sistered with Justice, Thou rulest and governest all things;
That we, honoured by Thee, may requite Thee with worship and honour,
Evermore praising thy works, as is meet for men that shall perish;
Seeing that none, be he mortal or God, hath privilege nobler
Than without stint, without stay, to extol Thy Law universal.

www.ingramcontent.com/pod-product-compliance
Lightning Source LLC
Chambersburg PA
CBHW021950160426
43195CB00011B/1303